Your First Tattoo

By

Linda Larson

A B C D E F

G H I J K L

M N O P Q R

S T U V W

X Y Z

A B C D E F G H

I J K L M N O P Q

R S T U V W X Y Z

So you want a tattoo ?

Now what ?

Here are some steps you can take to ensure you have a great experience

Research part 1

Figure out what you would like to get tattooed .

Tattoo artist's are not mind readers !

(I know shocking right ?)

These are amazing people with amazing art skills who want to make your dream come true ... still not mind readers .

Research what you would like to have tattooed . Even better find a picture for reference ! This is a great help to the tattoo artist in knowing what you are expecting .

This is going to be on your body forever !

So chose wisely .

Research Part 2

Now that you know what you would like to get tattooed , where are you going to put it ?

Be aware that if your tattoo has a lot of small details it will have to be a fair size to show all work (to much detail in to small of a place will eventually blur out ... I know by experience)

Listen to your artist !

If they suggest putting the tattoo a different place .. Take a minute and listen . They are trying to pick the best place to make your tattoo piece look the best . Not only that , they might worry about the amount of pain in some spots .

Your tattoo artist is your friend .

Research Part 3

What artist is going to do your tattoo ?

Every artist has their own style of work .

Ask around

Check out artists portfolios

Ask price

Location

You will find the artist you are looking for and have a much better experience

Of course you can be spontaneous and do a walk in . These appointments are on the fly and are usually smaller pieces . I have done this a few times ... however I already had a pretty good idea of what I wanted to get.

Tattoo Pain Chart

- Small Pin Pricks

- Cat Scratches

- Paper Cuts or Blow Torch

  Your Gonna need Something to Bite
  (Preferably not your friends hand)

- You may Cry. You may pass out.
  This is all acceptable.

- Your coffin.

Please note that this chart is relative to the person
getting the tattoo. If you have had one before, you
may not experience as much pain. A lot of it is
psychological, so being in a good mood an distracted
properly is the best way to handle getting a tattoo.

Think about it this way. Getting a tattoo for the first
time is gonna hurt, but the pain is only short lived
compared to the life long love for it.
IF YOU CHOOSE WISELY

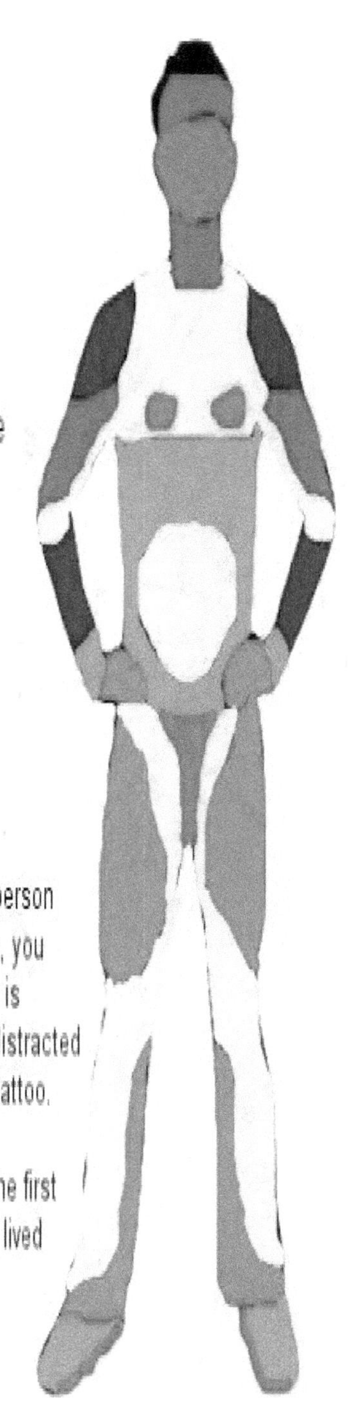

Make your Appointment !!

Be well aware that where ever you are getting tattooed will be sore for a day or so

(depends on the person)

So having to wear clothes over your new ink

(rubs the tattoo)

Being out in the sun

(feels like you are on fire)

Even sleep can be interrupted with a new tattoo .

I have gotten leg pieces that have made it impossible to drive for a day or two ...

Make plans and prepare for healing

Tattoo Day

Today is the day !!
Be on time !

When you arrive you will fill out your information for the artist on a waiver form .

The artist will set up the area (be patient)

Next comes the stencil & placement .

Once your stencil is on you ... take a look ... make sure it is how you would like it . The artist might be unhappy with how it looks and decide to clean it off and replace with a fresh stencil .

They use rubbing alcohol to clean the area of your tattoo .

Sometimes the artist might even shave the spot . Any fine hairs can be a problem with it comes to tattooing .

Breathe !!

Grab a seat in the artists chair (or table) depending on what area of your body you are getting tattooed .

Don't panic .

BREATHE

No need to get all worked up .

It is exciting getting Ink (especially your first) no need to panic .

Lets be straight . It does hurt , more stinging then anything . Different levels of pain depending where you get it and your pain tolerance .

BREATHE

Bring ear buds to listen to music or watch a show on your phone ..

Bring a friend (if allowed)

Some tattoo artists are chatty

Close your eyes and dream of how great your tattoo is going to look

You have got this !!

Welcome

To The

World Of

INK

Congratulations !!!

Take this moment to get a picture of your new tattoo . Some artists take their own pictures for their portfolios. Take a good look before it gets covered up for healing .

The artist will give your tattoo a rub down and then cover it .

It is a open wound.

Leave the bandage on for how long your artist says .

This helps bacteria from entering the wound .

Your artist will also give you instructions for aftercare of your new ink ... please read and follow . Not only will you heal better you are insuring this piece of art you just paid for looks great when healed .

Get Prepared

Tattoos are like chips .
You can not just eat (get) one .
So get prepared for wanting
more ink in the future .
Trust me (I have lost count of
how many tattoos I have)

Welcome the

to the Ink

world .

KEEP
CALM
AND
TATTOO
ON

Other Titles By Linda Larson

Tattooed People

Tattooed People #2

Tattooed People #3

My Weed Bible

Jewels of Italy

Peace, Love & Prayer

Thank you

Thank you for reading
Your First Tattoo .
I hope this book not
only gave you some
insight into your
decision but also left
you with a smile on
your face .
Please take a minute to
leave a review /
rating . This really
helps us as author's to
get out there .
Thank you

Linda Larson

A B C D E F

G H I J K L

M N O P Q R

S T U V W

X Y Z

A B C D E F G H

I J K L M N O P Q

R S T U V W X Y Z

www.ingramcontent.com/pod-product-compliance
Lightning Source LLC
Chambersburg PA
CBHW061550250726

48657CB00006B/2397